A GARDEN'S BLESSINGS

A GARDEN'S BLESSINGS

Refreshment For The Soul

LOIS TRIGG CHAPLIN

Augsburg

MINNEAPOLIS

A GARDEN'S BLESSINGS
Refreshment for the Soul

Scripture texts unless otherwise noted are from the New Revised Standard Version Bible, copyright ©1989 by the Division of Christian Education of the National Council of the Churches of Christ in the United States of America. Used with permission.

Photos by Van Chaplin and Beth Maynor, originally published in *Everyday Flowers* by Longstreet Press, Atlanta, Georgia, 1990.

Cover and interior design: Peggy Lauritsen Design Group

Library of Congress Cataloging-in-Publication Data
Chaplin, Lois Trigg.
    A garden's blessings : refreshment for the soul / Lois Trigg
Chaplin
       p. cm.
    ISBN 0-8066-2680-1 (alk. paper)
    1. Nature—Religious aspects—Christianity—Meditations.
    2. Gardens—Religious aspects—Christianity—Meditations.
    3. Chaplin, Lois Trigg. I. Title.
    BT695.5.C436 1993   93-5596
    242—dc20   CIP

The paper used in this publication meets the minimum requirements of American National Standard for Information Sciences—Permanence of Paper for Printed Library Materials, ANSI Z329.48-1984.

Manufactured in the U.S.A.   AF 9-2680
97   96   95   94   2   3   4   5   6   7   8   9   10

*To Van, Henry, Vandiver, Sarah,
Esmirna, and Vandalyn, to whom I owe
the happy fullness of each day. To Dad and
Uncle Raymond, who guided me as a young vine.
And to Robert and Anna Lou Marvin,
whose love of people and God's earthly designs
encouraged Van and me early in our
marriage and our careers.*

PREFACE

In my work as a garden writer, I am fortunate to spend many days walking and talking with people in their gardens, learning of their inner selves through their horticultural creations. How is it, I've pondered, that so diverse a social group can be so similar in spirit? Regardless of social stature, gender, or race, and no matter what burdens or handicaps they carry, gardeners exude happiness, enthusiasm, simplicity, and peace.

While reading the book of Genesis one day, I suddenly understood the reason why: "Then the Lord God formed man from the dust of the ground, and breathed into his nostrils the breath of life; and the man became a living being" (Genesis 2:7). Of course. The ground is a part of us, and we a part of it. Every gardener I've ever known would tell you that after a terrible day, digging in the earth lifts the tension and soothes the soul. Gardening is something we feel compelled to do. Indeed, through the soil we are in communion with God. Is it no wonder that gardeners are tranquil souls?

The next verse, Genesis 2:8, cemented my thoughts: "And the Lord God planted a garden in Eden, in the east; and there he put the man whom he had formed." God could have put us on a beach, on a mountain, in a desert, or in the ocean. But he chose to plant a garden especially for us. God is the original Gardener. Those of us who know the joys of a garden have a deep understanding of where we are meant to be. By bare-handedly working the earth and tending its fruits, we better know the Creator.

Just as almost every gardener I've met was influenced at a young age by another gardener, our human race was marked in its youth by God's first garden. As time and technology pull us farther from Eden's roots, a growing segment of our population feels lost, looking to drugs, cults, gangs, humanism, and other ill substitutes for the real God, and for the simple communion intended through our link with God's earth.

We don't have to journey to the Alps or the Amazon to feel the power of God's creation. It's in our own backyards—in the soil, water, trees, flowers, and air. The closer we look and wonder, the more we know. In the architecture of an ant, God's presence is revealed. But how many of us really look? My hope is that through this little book, you will see the plants and creatures of the garden, and beyond them their Creator.

If you are a gardener or have a love for nature, I trust that you will identify with the meditations I have written—I know you could add many more drawn from your own experience. And if you are not a gardener, I hope you will be moved to plant a tomato, a tree, or a pot of flowers—or at least share in the joy of somebody else's. After all, sharing—the giving of the firstfruits (either literally or spiritually) is really what gardening is all about.

A GARDEN'S BLESSINGS

A *gift from God takes many forms, each according to the recipient, but to all of us has been given one gift in common: a garden. Through it we come to understand more about God and ourselves, and that you and I are but a tiny part of a much larger scheme.*

A Personal Story

I was born in Havana, Cuba, in 1954—a time when the city was at its peak with nightlife, casinos, and American business, and was the seat of Latin American culture. We lived on the fifth floor of a shiny, white condominium complex—*Soledad*—overlooking Havana Bay. I remember how pristine it was, washed by fresh sea air and having floors of highly waxed terrazzo. You could spot its gleaming exterior and art-deco scalloped corridors from the Malecon—Havana's bay-front boardwalk. In a country of harsh economic contrasts it was a clean, prestigious place to live.

Except for school days, when I wore my blue uniform, my mother would dress me in organza and other lacy, itchy frocks. Needless to say, I never touched dirt. My mother was the quintessential Cuban city woman. Her nails were long and polished. Her clothes were stylish, and her lips were always painted red. To my mother, dirt under the fingernails was synonymous with a life of farming and, likely, poverty. She took care to guard her fair Spanish skin from sun, too—and naturally, she guarded mine. Gardening was not part of our household routine.

Then on October 7, 1960, life changed dramatically. We left Havana and moved to a single-wide, one-bedroom trailer in Garden City, Florida (now part of Jacksonville). My father, who is American, had to flee Cuba's new communist regime. The trailer belonged to my uncle, who had lived in it while building his retirement home in the country. There we set up what we thought would be temporary housekeeping, waiting for Castro to be removed. And although the trailer was

In a garden, we work the soil of which we are a part. Life was created from the elements—and by digging the soil and working in the rains, the sun, and the wind, the vigor of nature is upon our skin. "You are dust, and to dust you shall return" (Genesis 3:19).

Ever wonder why children, when left to their
visceral selves, are at home in the dirt?
It's instinctual. There is no fear, only the
urge to play, to explore.

cramped and unglamorous, the acres surrounding it
opened a new world to me.

In those north Florida pine flatwoods I
learned to roast hot dogs pierced with palmetto stick
"handles" over an open fire, to chase frogs and grab lizards

by the tail, and to swing from live oak branches on a long rope with a soft, dangling seat fashioned from a burlap sack stuffed with Spanish moss.

I'll never forget my first encounter with the screech of an owl in the night. I yelled, "Momma!" while running from my living room sofa bed to the other end of the trailer where my parents slept. (In retrospect, it would have been much wiser to yell for Daddy, who was raised on the edge of the Okefenokee Swamp.) My poor city-lights-and-action mother was still adjusting to the rural stillness. "This country is so dark," she would say. "I don't know why they don't put streetlights out here."

I also discovered fire ants—one of the negatives of my new world. But there were many intriguing, friendly ants, too—the kind you could watch going in and out of their mound while you lay on your stomach just a breath away. They would climb over my arms and legs nonchalantly, and I wondered what it was like to live in a mound.

My father took me through the woods to walk the creek, and showed me how to cut a small gash in the trunk of a tree as he did when he was a kid. There we would later harvest some sweet gum. Until then all my gum had come in wrappers.

My aunt grew pink poppies, whose dry seedpods rattled, and with all the delight of a kid with a saltshaker, I would turn the dried pods sideways to shake out the tiny seeds. Eventually the poppy stand grew so large it was spotted from overhead by a helicopter. My sweet aunt's flowers happened to be the same type as the ones harvested for opium, and the narcotics officers in the copter told her they had to go.

My uncle had an old, red tractor, and one of my most vivid memories is of walking along behind it, digging and lifting sweet potatoes from the soil churned by the tines. Each potato was a mystery: Where was it? How big was it? What shape would it be? Nothing could be more fun for a six-year-old.

Within a few short months there was plenty of dirt under my fingernails—and elsewhere, too. The move from urban Havana to country life in Garden City quickly made me a gardener, someone very much aware of God's creation. Garden City showed me the complex simplicity of nature, and how each creature has a place—even the big, black roach I found hiding in my shoe. ◕

LESSONS FROM A FLOWER

I don't recall ever hearing anyone say, "I hate flowers." Quite the contrary, the universal phrase is: "I love flowers." Even those of us who never garden enjoy the blossoms of a friend's garden, or flowers as a gift. There is awe in a bloom, a mysterious magnetism that

Every child deserves a chance to know a bean plant from a pea; to discover bumblebees sleeping in the salvia; to realize that seeds sprout, grow, and die in their own time; and to learn the patient example of branches that lengthen and grow stronger, bit by bit.

fixes a gaze. The scent of a blossom is the same way. We pluck a flower and put it up to our nose again and again. There is no getting enough of it.

In the biblical story of creation, God said, "Let the earth put forth vegetation: plants yielding seed, and fruit trees of every kind on earth that bear fruit with the seed in it" (Genesis 1:11). And to bear seed, very simply, God made flowers—each in its own kind, with a beauty and diversity that define nature. Today, when plant taxonomists classify plants, they do so primarily by the structure of the flower. Sometimes a flower yields the only clue for distinguishing species that in other ways appear identical.

How quickly we gardeners come to see the ecological significance of flowers, and blooms begin to speak to us in ordinary ways. We see the peeping of a daffodil as a declaration of spring. We hear the brown blotches on a should-be-white gardenia screaming, "A brood of thrips is hiding in my folds!" We watch the red, trumpet-shaped blossoms call the hummingbirds; the blue ones call the bees. And four-o'clocks tell us it's time to go in and cook supper. Indeed, flowers are the metronome of life. Without them there would be no trees for oxygen, no leaves to build the fertile soil, and no roots to hold it together. No animals. No food chain. No grain. No us.

Blossoms are the essence of God's gift of life on earth, and we gardeners get to bring them from seed to fruition, in all their variety. And we see that as different as each kind may be, they all proclaim the eternity, intelligence, and grace of their Creator. ❧

In the book of Genesis you need read no further than Eden to conclude that the outdoors is our natural home. It is ironic that we spend thousands of dollars on comforts for our air-conditioned abodes, and even cultivate plants indoors, but many of us don't consider spending the same on the room just outside our door.

Peony and yellow columbine

"Every flower of the field, every fiber of a plant,
every particle of an insect, carries with it
the impress of its Maker, and can—if duly
considered—read us lectures of ethics or divinity"
(Thomas Pope Blount).

God's Fingerprints

It has been said that the universe is like a safe to which there is a combination, but the combination is locked up in the safe. By looking closely at my garden, I feel I can see inside the safe, and I see intriguing sets of threes—trinities—and perhaps the fingerprint of a Creator with a sense of allegory and even humor.

In first grade we learn about the three basic categories: animal, vegetable, or mineral. My garden is composed of vegetable matter and the mineral soil that supports all life. As for animals, they'll serenade me or feast on my crops. Either way, their presence is undeniable.

Another trinity stamped upon the earth is in the soil. How quickly a garden will teach us the importance of building rich, fertile soil from one of God's three types—sand, silt, or clay. Jesus gave us the parable of the sower (Mark 4:3-9) to teach us a spiritual truth based on the productiveness of the soil.

Perhaps water is the matter that matters most to us gardeners, and it takes all three of matter's forms: solid, liquid, and gas. In its icy, solid form we fear the weight it bears on tree branches or how it can heave our plants from the soil. Flowing water will carry life from the roots of a garden to its very top, or it can drown it unmercifully. And as a gas, humidity will bring some plants to their knees with disease, yet be the synergist of fast growth for others.

In the sky we look to the sun, the moon, and the stars. We place our plants according to their need for sunlight so that they may feed themselves by day and grow well at night. During the day the butterflies visit, and in the moonlight we find moths bringing pollen for the seeds of life.

These recurring "trinities" in the building blocks of my garden make me think that if God—Father, Son, and Holy Spirit—left fingerprints, they may be revealed here. When Christ was training his disciples, he said that to them "has been given the secret of the kingdom of God, but for those outside, everything comes in parables" (Mark 4:11). Perhaps nature itself is the sum of many living parables, and with a sharp sense of humor, God has plopped us down right in the midst of them. ❧

When parents spend time sowing seeds with their children, they are actually sowing seeds of a much larger kind. Children in a garden ask questions and do things you never thought they had in them. "What we are is God's gift to us. What we become is our gift to God"
(Eleanor Powell).

It's fun *to talk about grandma's flowers and discover snails and shuck corn and delight in a moonflower as it instantly unfurls; to learn the clockwork of a morning glory and smell the honeysuckle on a sultry night.*

❧

THE BEE, THE WASP, AND THE BUTTERFLY

There is an old saying that has been popularized in garden plaques and in many other ways because it rings so true: "One's heart is closer to God in a garden than anywhere else on earth." I believe that God sometimes uses that sense of closeness to offer us the most personal and unexpected insights—often through the very plants and creatures we gardeners dearly love. For me, one of my garden's fascinations has been watching the insects that live there go to and fro in their own subworld. I've long felt a kinship with bugs, but there was one day when that link became especially significant for me.

When I was about eight months pregnant with our first son, a bumblebee landed on my stomach. I shook him off, and not thinking much more about it, I filed the incident away in my memory.

Two years later, while pregnant with our second son, a big, red wasp flew onto my pregnant belly. Again, I shook it off, though admittedly with a greater sense of urgency, as wasps are easily provoked.

Four years later, when I was pregnant with our third child, a butterfly came to light on my rotund womb. Immediately, the bee and wasp incidents were relived: two stingers and a butterfly. At that moment I was sure that after two boys, our third child would be a girl. (And I was right.)

Some may laugh at me for seeing these events as a personal message from God, but I don't mind. As that butterfly flew away, I knew better than ever that God is indeed very personal, and I should never underestimate his ways. This time, God's angels had six legs. ❧

The garden is
the best room of the
house. It's enriching,
mysteriously spiritual,
and kinetic. A slice of
creation, it kindles the
simple pleasures.

SAND OR CLAY?

At one time or another most of us have molded a creation from potter's clay. The clay we use comes from the ground, like the clay of our garden soil. All clay is made up of microscopic mineral layers that soak up water like a sponge. When moistened to the proper consistency, clay will take whatever form we give it, shaped by the talents of its sculptor. When the clay loses water it becomes hard and brittle and must be handled gingerly to avoid breaking. Yet if baked in the heat of fire, it becomes stronger and holds its shape.

On the other hand, sand holds little water. Its small, hard grains refuse to bind into a malleable mass. Each grain is really a tiny piece of rock, impenetrable, with no interspacial layers and little capacity for water. How easily our summer sand castles are broken because of the sand's inability to absorb the glue that is water.

Today I can watch the red clay in my Alabama garden steadfastly clutch water, and I remember the sands of my Florida garden that let it slip away. I have watched beans and tomatoes go limp as their roots could find no water in the sand. Likewise, I have seen the same crops drink water and thrive in a soil rich in water-loving clay. On the same kind of hot day, each of us gardeners has thirsted and found relief in a glass of iced water.

One day Christ thirsted and asked for water from a Samaritan woman at a well (John 4:7-15). Then the conversation shifted, and it was he who was offering *her* some water—living water—so that her soul would not thirst. As a gardener, I know that water is the life of my plants and my body. It is easy to see how Christ, the living water, is the life of my soul.

Will we, like clay, soak up that living water so there is growth in our spiritual garden, or do we, like impenetrable sand, hold little water and let our spirits wilt in the heat of the day? ❧

It's heartbreaking to spade an earthworm in half or watch your favorite flower fade, but the garden gives promise that the earthworm will regenerate, and the flower will return the next day or the next year.

*Gardening calls on our God-given emotion
and creativity. In the garden, God speaks to our
bodies and spirits. We feel. We learn. We
sweat. We grow stronger. We heal. We nurture.
In both a spiritual sense and practical sense,
we reap what we sow.*

LIKE A TREE

On the forest floor a stately tree began life
as a tiny seed buried in darkness. After a cold winter,
spring lit and warmed its leafy bed, and the water of life
touched the seed. It sprouted, and patiently and silently it
sent a tender young stem up through the soft leaves that

had been its shelter since fall. Later, brambles and weeds tried to block the way, but the young seedling carried on.

The baby tree directed its growth toward the light, growing a bit taller and stronger with each warm season. Some years it grew more than others. The growth rings of its trunk tell the story of fertile years and poor years. Patiently it persisted in spite of droughts and frosts that threatened its growth. After several decades the tree broke through the canopy of the forest, atop a trunk made strong by layers of experience.

Now its branches stretch far and wide, and every leaf bathes in the light to make food. Each fall the mature tree gives its leaves to the earth to make a fertile bed for new seedlings.

When the blind man at Bethsaida who was healed by Jesus used his eyes for the very first time, he said he saw men, but they looked like trees walking (Mark 8:22-24). Although the blind man had never seen either a man or a tree, he knew them nevertheless. Not hindered by the blinders of vision, he had seen the tree in all of us. ॐ

SOIL OR DIRT?

It is curious how we have come to call the ground "dirt." Decades ago, when we made our living from the land and were obviously closer to it, we "soiled" our clothes, but now we get them "dirty." Items sold below value are "dirt cheap." And a distasteful chore or a deceit is "dirty work."

Lima bean

A nutritious vegetable becomes so much more.
We learn to appreciate it as a seed, as a seedling,
and as a mature crop. It is freshly made by
our efforts and the grace of God.

How many children are rebuked at an early age for getting dirty? Yet if left to their own, the measure of the day's fun would be the size of the grimy rings in the folds of their necks. I once heard a friend say that her nephew's idea of entertainment and fun always had a price attached—movies, lunch out, wacky golf, video arcades, and the like. Perhaps he never had the freedom to grub around in the soil as most children would innately do. Maybe children are closer to the origins that we adults no longer feel.

Genesis tells us that in the beginning God molded man from a handful of clay. It could have happened in a few minutes, or God could have worked the clay for eons. In God's own time I'll know the answers to such questions. But what I know now is that if you burn my body in a crucible, it will yield the elemental ashes of the earth. Each fall I sprinkle extra iron on the soil around my azaleas to give color and energy to their leaves. The same element also gives color and oxygen to my blood.

God is the potter and I am the clay. The soil runs through my veins, and when my finger presses against the earth I am a blood brother with creation. ☙

RENEWAL

This morning I walked out my front door
into a whorl of warm wind from the Gulf that brings a fall
rain and whisks red and yellow leaves from the trees all
around me. Everywhere wet and matted leaves make the
street, driveway, and walks slippery. Yet I can walk with
confidence in this place I know so well. Leaves carpet my
neighbors' porches, their lawns, and their once-neat
flower beds. In my backyard it is hard to tell where the
raised beds of the vegetable garden end for the depth of
the leaves. And my dwarf yaupons have leaves wedged
between their branches that will have to be plucked out
one by one. For a moment the leafy rain seems a nuisance,
turning my summer-neat garden into a littered mess.

But with more steps into the rattle and
roar of the leaves resisting the wind, I rejoice in what a
glorious time of renewal this is. Although the juggle of
family, home, and career have left me feeling as though I
just finished spring planting, that doesn't matter today.

Just a few days ago these same leaves that
are raining down around me were like a watercolor against
the sky. I doubt it is a coincidence that leaves are brightest
when they are exhausted by having given all they can give,
and their color most brilliant when penetrated by light.
Today the dry leaves that rest on the ground hold the life

that will be my garden's resurrection. They will return nutrients to the soil so that other plants might live. And every year the cycle is repeated—life from death—as nature echoes the promise of Christ. ❧

Bunch grapes

A banquet of flavors and sounds and scents
is ours. We pucker at an unripe grape, cry in the
fumes of an onion, savor the subtlety of chives,
inhale the juicy-fruit sweetness of tea olive,
and respond to the rattle of Crotalaria *when its*
seeds call to be gathered.

In a garden we feel
the breeze of a bee and
follow the flotations
of a butterfly.

LIKE CORN, LIKE ME

On one of the many occasions my
uncle Raymond and I shucked corn together, he said to
me: "You know, Lois, if you count the silks and kernels
on that ear, their number will be the same." Well, to a
nine-year-old that was tantamount to learning of the
sparkle emitted from Wintergreen Life Savers when you
bite down on them in a dark closet. Immediately I
picked up a new ear of corn and began to dissect it,
one tassel at a time.

When you're only nine, it's no easy
task to keep up with each tassel and the count in your
head, too. Corn silks are very fine and hard to handle,
and more than once I had to start over with the pile of
silks I carefully laid out on the picnic table. Next I count-
ed kernels, marking each with a poke of my nail as I
worked first up and then down the ear. In about two
hours I finished (with my uncle's help), and the count,
which I don't remember exactly, was so close that I
knew he must be right. Suddenly I thought of the many
ears of corn I'd shucked or eaten in ignorance of such
fabulous knowledge.

Many years later I read in Matthew and
Luke where a reassuring Christ told his anxious disciples
that even the hairs on their heads were numbered. That

line sprang off the page at me. After years of studying biology, zoology, botany, genetics, and other sciences in school, I now have no doubt that every hair in the universe is numbered. Yet the ear of corn from the garden had showed me the same thing long ago. ❧

Tomato

Subtleties are paramount with our favorite:
tomatoes. Like connoisseurs of fine wine,
we debate back and forth as to which variety
is the best.

Early goldenrod, Black-eyed Susan, Sunflower 'Taiyo', English ivy, Rye-grass

To a gardener, flowers are as alive indoors as they are out. To paraphrase a friend, gardeners don't arrange flowers, we just gather them in a vase to celebrate them as we found them.

GARDEN FUNERALS

Every season we gardeners hold countless little funerals. Season after season, as we go about a garden's daily business, we see, feel, and smell a thousand little deaths:

• Vegetables produce their harvest and the plants are killed by frost. We lay them in the compost to be transformed into a "gardener's gold."

• A spade turns up the carcass of a ground beetle. We turn the beetle back into the soil.

• An expired honeybee lies beneath the fertilized squash blossoms. We leave him to his environment—like a sailor buried at sea.

• A small fly is stuck, paralyzed, in a stringy web. We see the meal of a spider.

• The cat delivers a dead chipmunk to the back door. We bury it by the apple tree to serve as fertilizer.

• A flower shrivels with age. We watch it wither, and later we collect next year's seed.

In our daily toil such little deaths seem hardly to be a death at all, but rather a moment in the life of a garden, a flicker in its flame. Death in a garden is an expected and essential aspect of existence. How healthy it would be if we could accept our own mortality in the same way—and in the hope that when we must wither, we will have produced our fruit, our seed, and a rich spiritual compost for those we leave behind. ᜷

Eastern sycamore (*Platanus occidentalis*)

We are made to pause at the majesty of a tree.

LIVING WATER

The first thing a gardener does after sowing seeds or setting out new plants is to give them water. Without it, seeds lie fallow and plants wither and die. We turn on a sprinkler or screw the water breaker nozzle on the hose end, literally baptizing our plants into their homes. At this point a gardener comes to know that he or she is but a third party exercising faith in the other two—the plant and its Creator.

Again and again through the season we deliver water between rains. We watch it bring life to dry, inert soil, and we see its power revive a wilted garden. In this way God makes it easy for us to understand Jesus when he said, "Those who drink of the water that I will give them will never be thirsty. The water that I will give will become in them a spring of water gushing up to eternal life" (John 4:14).

A gardener understands the undeniable power of a spring. ❧

O bserve the
parallels between the
laws of nature and the
realities of life. The
strong eat the weak.
Living things grow when
they are fed and decline
when they are not.
The dying return to the
earth. "For everything
there is a season. . . ."
(Ecclesiastes 3:1).

FAITH

A gardener works by faith, and often without conscious realization of it. As a kid I planted many a seed, covered them, watered them, waited for them to grow, and had a joyous time doing so. Did I have *faith* that the seed would soon become a plant? Not really. I first did it because my daddy showed me how and then because it was fun. I didn't connect it to "faith," that thing my Sunday school teachers talked about.

Nandina (*Nandina domestica*)

Despite the inconvenience to those in northern climes, a garden holds an undeniable quiet and beauty when cloaked in snow.

Faith came in adulthood, not in a single, shattering revelation, but slowly from within, to the point where I understood it enough to share it with others.

If you take aspects of gardening at their face value, they might seem pretty ridiculous to those who don't garden or who have never been close to a gardener. Consider the couple that braves a cold, late-winter day to drive many miles to their favorite garden center and spends more than a hundred dollars on a dozen brown sticks labeled "roses."

They quickly unload the brown sticks and plunge them into a tub of water to soak for a while. Then they dig twelve holes in soil that they have labored over each year, but which never seems quite perfect enough. In the past week they have doctored the soil further by turning in compost, cottonseed meal, bone meal, and other soil helps with a sturdy, solid-shank fork whose colorful coating is long-gone from use. Next they turn in three carts full of chopped leaves made last fall with the $300 shredder the kids gave them several Christmases ago.

At once each bare-root rose is painstakingly centered and shifted in its planting hole; the plant is positioned up and down a few times to get the level just right, and the roots groomed and coiffed like hair into their proper places. The level of the plant is crucial, for if the graft is buried, the rose could die. One of them holds the thorny top just so, while the other on his hands and knees refills the hole to cover the roots with soil. When the rose seems anchored in place it is let go, and the soil around it is firmly patted with the same gentle touch afforded to a baby's back end.

Next they shovel up more cartfuls of chopped leaves, evenly spreading them between the plants like icing on a cake. This is the mulch that will keep the soil cool in summer, warm in winter, moist in drought, and hopefully free of most weeds. Finally they drag out the coiled, winter-stiffened hose and hook up the sprinkler to give the sticks some water.

Then they walk away. They have done their part. Now God's earth and sun and rain will do theirs.

That's the faith and the trust of a gardener.

∞

*A garden provides a natural zoo filled with
fascinating creatures. Spiders become friends as we
work beside each other.*

WEEDS

In the whole scheme of things I would like to think that there are no weeds because somewhere on this earth every plant has a place and purpose in nature. But in a garden, where we each have a personal recipe for order with the trees, shrubs, flowers, herbs, fruits, and vegetables that we prefer, the uninvited plants sometimes give us trouble.

Horticulturists define a weed as a plant that is out of place. I like that. It allows much room for interpretation. Some of the prettiest yellow "wildflowers" I've ever seen were a spring crop of dandelions at Franklin Park in Columbus, Ohio. Their blooms were much bigger than dandelions make here in the South, and they carpeted the park with the grace of a field of sunflowers, seeming very much in their proper place. Yet in the manicured lawns across the street from the park, the dandelions roused my conditioning to view them as weeds.

Wild potato vines and dichondra are the most aggravating weeds in my garden. The dichondra undermines the "Bath's pinks" and creeping thyme, and I must chase their entangled strands through leaves, under stems, and around rhizomes, carefully prying the tenacious runners from the ground they attempt to steal from my plants. I know wild potato vines are nice in some garden spots, but in my garden most of them are "plants out of place." They sprout everywhere, climbing the tomatoes, lilies, salvia, sunflowers, and nandinas—anything that will give their flimsy, lecherous lengths support. I pull them and pull them, but again and again they resprout. Yet my persistence is ultimately greater than theirs.

On the surface, weeds aren't really welcomed in a garden, but in the end it is probably good that they are there. They cause us to look more closely at what we grow and force us to tend the garden more carefully, lest it be completely lost. Weeds can also remind

Common persimmon (*Diospyros virginiana*)

"There is no fruit that is not bitter before it is ripe" (Publius Syrus).

us of the greed, pride, deceit, anger, foolishness, and a thousand other human weaknesses that, if allowed to grow freely inside us, can choke our ability to bear fruit. ༺

A gardener gets excited about something as simple
as planting a pot of mixed flowers and
anticipating the outcome.

IN TRAINING

In my garden I have trained, coaxed, and pruned many vines—grapes, trumpet honeysuckle, moonvine, morning glory, clematis, roses, climbing fig, mandevilla, and others. Now that I am training, coaxing, and occasionally pruning three children, I often relive some of my encounters with vines, only in a human way.

My sons are like morning glories—up at dawn and full speed ahead. My daughter is a moonvine—

eyes shut in the morning but wide open at night. Yet morning glories and moonvines play out their lives in a short season, while a child will not grow to adulthood until many summers and winters have passed. Children are woody vines, like the grapes of the vineyard that will yield various measures of fruit, depending in large part on how they are trained. They send out shoots in all possible directions and depend on wise hands that can help them select the best leaders from among their own shoots. These shoots will then grow longer, thicker, stronger, and fruitful, unless a drastic pruning changes the vine's course and brings on a new harvest.

As it is with vines, so it often seems with children, and though a child is infinitely more valuable than a vine, any gardener who is also a parent can laugh and cry at the parallels between the two. "Train children in the right way, and when old, they will not stray" (Proverbs 22:6). ❧

Daffodil 'Ice Follies'

News of a new breed of daffodils with
extra-sturdy, weatherproof stems brings
experiment and could be the height of
the new garden season.

In a society, gardening is the great equalizer. It does not attach social meaning to rich or poor, black or white, city or country, white collar or blue collar, and the thousand other social categories humans create. A garden grows well for anyone who tends it well. "I think the King is but a man as I am; the violet smells to him as it doth to me" (William Shakespeare).

Sunflower 'Mixed' (*Helianthus annus*)

We can't wait to get home to see what bloom
might have opened today or which squash might
be big enough for picking. Then we take it all in
from a favorite garden spot. Forget the TV chair.

SEEDS OF LOVE

A caterpillar asks a cocoon, "Tell me, sir, what is a butterfly?"

The cocoon answers, "It is what you are meant to become. It flies with beautiful wings and joins the earth to heaven. It drinks only nectar from the flowers and carries the seeds of love from one flower to another."*

Botany teaches us that seeds won't form without pollen and without the help of the butterflies, bees, bats, wasps, beetles, moths, and ants that are nature's main instruments of delivery. Watching bees and butterflies unknowingly disperse life-giving pollen through their daily work reminds me how similar they are to humans. Every day, as we go about our routines, we land on other people's "flowers"—at home, at work, in our neighborhoods, and on the streets. Do we deliver God's pollen through our example and deeds?

In our communities we can volunteer for one of many worthwhile causes, or we can say we don't have time. At home, we can help prepare our children to take part in school, or we can pretend that education is only a teacher's job. In the anonymity of our cars, we can

*From *Hope for the Flowers* by Trina Paulus (New York: Paulist Press, 1972). Used by permission.

change lanes to allow another auto to merge, or we can choose to selfishly ignore the needs of the other driver.

The Gospels tell us that whoever would selfishly save his life will lose it, and whoever loses his life in Christ's work will find it. The bees, butterflies, and other carriers—tireless and directed—spread pollen as they go about their daily business, and the results are the seeds of life. They set a good example. ❧

LIGHT OF LIFE

We humans might take a cue from the way plants consistently and without exception seek light. Without light every living thing on earth would die, for the living world is dependent on the food that plants make by converting sunlight to energy. There is an African violet on my desk that turns its leaves on angle to best capture the sunlight streaming in the window. Every few days I give the pot a half turn so it won't get

We fashion with great ingenuity a sturdy trellis to support vines—and occasionally a visitor.

too lopsided, yet a day or two later, the leaves are all prone to the window again. It never falters.

In our world light makes all things visible. It is the swift messenger by which we can distinguish between tiny atoms and measure the distances to the planets and stars. Every flower in our gardens—indeed, everything on earth—owes its color to the way it reflects or absorbs light.

Jesus said, "I am the light of the world. Whoever follows me will never walk in darkness but will have the light of life" (John 8:12). Our eyes can see how light gives life and vibrancy to the world around us. Will our inner spirits be open to and illuminated by the Light of life? ❧

Flowering quince (Chaenomeles speciosa)

We never stop trying new varieties as well as the
old varieties we've never grown before.

↶

PASS-ALONG SPIRIT

When our oldest son Henry was between
three and four years old, he would share with us his new-
found interpretations of the world. One of my favorites
was, "In tennis you serve the ball, but you don't eat it."

Another definition I will never forget is: "When you're sick you can give it to somebody and still keep it." That one must have churned around in his mind for a while. At the age of three or four, a child is just beginning to understand the concept of sharing and must sometimes be pushed into giving things over, even for just a few minutes. Then something comes along that you can have, give away, and keep all at the same time. Sounds great, except it's a virus.

Henry's definition applies to gardening, too. The spirit of gardening is giving and keeping, for if we give, we always receive. A bed of daylilies or iris will stop blooming, but when the crowded plants are divided and the extras given away, the flowers flourish again. Sometimes long after a gardener has given away a start of a plant, the mother plant dies. Then the gardener must get a new start from the plant that was shared. Today many favorite old plants are around only because of generations of sharing. Felder Rushing, my county-agent friend in Jackson, Mississippi, has a term for such plants. He calls them "pass-along plants." They've been kept in cultivation only by the passing along of family and friends.

Gardeners have a pass-along spirit, too. Every year a good portion of my garden consists of plants shared by other gardeners—like a living quilt of precious memories and friendships. ❧

*Like one's preference for an old and familiar
bed pillow, a gardener gets attached to worn
but faithful, useful equipment.*

As caretakers
of God's big room,
gardeners appreciate
comforts for living
outdoors. Though made
by human hands, we
see in them their real
source—God-given
talents and ingenuity.
We see beauty in the
simple things and
things often taken
for granted.

Gardening isn't hoarding. As part of God's providence, plants inherently call us to share. When the harvest overwhelms, we welcome takers. When plants become crowded, we divide them to share with any and all, or the plants decline. "It is more blessed to give than to receive" (Acts 20:35).

TIME OUT

This morning I saw my neighbor on his knees before a bed of rich, black soil that is the dream of every gardener, so I walked over to say hello and ask about the pansies he had planted a few weeks ago. John is retired, and his circle of friends and activities don't overlap mine, yet gardening gives us much in common. As I greeted him, John remained on his knees, shoveling his much-worked beautiful soil with a curious short-handled shovel. That shovel could probably tell the story of his whole gardening life. While we talked, he dug, preparing a bed for tulip bulbs.

That's the thing about gardening—one always feels free to talk and work at the same time, and often the work leads to yet another topic of conversation. In this case, I first admired the deep, friable, organic soil John has "been working on for years." That led to his offering me loads of chopped leaves, of which he had a big surplus. That may not mean much to some folks, but to a gardener, it's the ultimate offering, and one of mutual understanding—like loaning a friend a very good book. Even better, John's leaves had already been lovingly ground into fine little pieces!

After gladly accepting the offer, I asked John more about the short little spade with which he dug so comfortably, as if in the company of an old friend. It was a WW II GI issue entrenching tool, very sturdy and still dependable despite years of use. The handle was less than two feet long, a perfect length for spading from your knees, and the shank pivoted so the blade could fold up to fit in a knapsack. When I asked him how old the tool was,

We even find a way to make good of a strip of old pantyhose.

John turned the spade up and rubbed the soil from the blade to uncover the date, 1944. He'd never noticed that before. The tool led to talk of the war and the sacrifice that it was for all, and of the hell it must have been to dig a trench for a bed at night. And I wondered what man might have first clutched that shovel to dig his underground bed so that I might tonight sleep peacefully in mine. John talked of his days as a pilot in the European theater. They got shot up pretty badly a couple of times, but he "always managed to get 'er back on the ground."

We talked of politics, taxes, and the deficit, and of how God gives us leeway in our choices. And, oh yes, the pansies. They hadn't all grown as he expected them to, and together we determined it was a lack of light. Right down the middle of the bed there was a band of pansies that looked healthy enough, but they were only half the size of the rest of the plants. The trunk of a distant but tall Southern red oak from the neighbor's yard cast a long shadow in the low angle of the autumnal sun that darkened these pansies just enough to keep them small.

It would have been easy to bypass John on this hectic morning. I had just returned from car pool—and the school, the post office, the grocery, and the bank. That evening there would be homework, basketball practice, supper, a gift to wrap, and a call from the insurance man. At that moment I had been much pressed to get the milk and eggs into the refrigerator and get to work on the manuscript for this book—but thank God, taking care of a garden absolutely requires that you clock out. And when I stepped over the short wall that separates our place from John's, the balance in my day was restored. I would share with my neighbor, and he with me. And when I stepped back across the wall, I had been given pause enough to handle the rest of the day. ❧

All gardeners—no matter what our age—
remember when and where we first gardened. An
act as ordinary as giving water to a plant is so
crucial to our being that its memory grows brighter
through the years. Every flower, every weed, every
fruit, every creature from God's garden can—
through beauty or its challenge—give us a greater
appreciation for the Creator. "Ask the plants of
the earth, and they will teach you" (Job 12:8).

TO TILL IT AND KEEP IT

While the term *mutual symbiosis* may
sound like some exotic disease, it is actually the scientific
term for two organisms that live together for the benefit
of both. In simple terms, it is a win/win situation.

Among the most beautiful examples of
such symbiosis in nature is a lichen—a body of algae and
fungi woven into one. In every lichen there is a colony
of alga that makes food for the fungus in exchange for
shelter inside the fungus's protective sheath. Lichens are
remarkably cosmopolitan, both in the diverse combina-
tions of algal and fungal species, and in their geograph-
ical spread from deserts to the Arctic to the deepest valleys
to Alpine peaks.

Yet for me the most remarkable example
of mutual symbiosis is one we take for granted—the bio-
logical relationship God established between humans and
plants. We breathe what plants exhale (oxygen), and they
breathe what we exhale (carbon dioxide). Together we live
in a continual state of mutual CPR.

Even more, perhaps we share something
deeper than an organic symbiosis with plants, but a primal
connection as well. Remember, "the Lord God took the
man and put him in the garden of Eden to till it and keep
it" (Genesis 2:15). Eventually Adam and Eve were evicted,

but we gardeners are still tilling it and keeping it. Perhaps it is the inhaling and the exhaling, and the nurturing between us and our gardens—for a garden nurtures us as much as we it—that brings us the peace and joy of our lost Eden, the memory of home. ᴧ

Peanut butter and petunias. The author takes a
break with daughter Sarah.